What I Meant When I Said I'm Fine

Poems by Hazel Gahagan

Dedicated with love to

Team Gahgs

Contents

"Oh please, don't ask me how I've been, don't make me play pretend..."

- Fake Happy (Paramore)

What I Meant When I Said I'm Fine

"How are you?"
"I'm fine."

It becomes a reflex after a while. The longer you haven't been "fine", the faster the response falls out of your mouth.

But what does "fine" mean? It meant so many things to me, but none of them could really be described as "fine".

"Fine" was a buffer; protection from having to tell someone, anyone, how I really felt. They wouldn't want to hear it, I told myself. The truth is, I didn't want them to know. Or to judge.

Since my teens, I have been (in some way or another) under the mental health system. Diagnoses came and went, but the problems never left. Depression, anxiety, borderline personality disorder, avoidant personality disorder, mixed personality disorder (PD-NOS), complex-PTSD, agoraphobia, social anxiety disorder, mixed anxiety and depressive disorder, and now in my thirties, finding out that I am autistic, my list of previous and current diagnoses feel like random guesses made by disinterested psychiatrists who decided my fate based on shallow, ten-minute conversations. Throw in my fibromyalgia diagnosis and I feel like nothing more than a list of things that are wrong with me.

But in all honesty, it's not about the diagnoses.

This collection of poems spans the past several years of my life – namely my mid-twenties to early-thirties. Amongst the chaos of the mental health system and the multitude of diagnoses, the one constant was that I was forever trying to hide the pain I was feeling.

Whether it was fear of being judged, fear of being vulnerable, fear of losing people, or fear of losing the idea of "me" that I had crafted, I spent years answering the question "How are you?" with "Fine thanks, you?" Even with mental health professionals, in appointments where I was supposed to talk about myself, I would give the same response. I would try to divert the conversation onto them, to distract them from asking about me.

I didn't want to admit my pain. It was too hard, too messy, too much. I didn't want to be That Person… whatever that meant. I convinced myself that when people asked, "How are you?" they didn't really care to hear the answer. They wanted me to say, "Fine thanks, you?" and be done with the pleasantries.

But people did care. Still, to this day, I struggle not to revert to my old friend "fine", but it's a difficult habit to break. But now, my loved ones know my secret – they know my "fine" routine. When I respond with "Fine thanks", they reply with "Are you fine-fine, or Hazel-fine?" (Meaning: not really fine).

It's such a small thing but asking this clarifying question has been a game-changer for me.

It's like being reassured: Hey, I actually want to know how you are. It's safe to tell me. I have time to listen and you're not a burden.

Things are getting better. I'm learning and growing every day; about myself and the world. Opening up has been a big part of that and these poems represent all those thoughts and feelings that stayed hidden behind "Fine" for so long.

This is what I meant when I said, "I'm fine".

Trapped

The air feels oppressive
And I don't mean the heat
My feet tap, legs twitch
Like an itch I cannot reach
And my hands, they tremble
Like my soul might eject from my body
And crack this veneer I've held dear
Like a crayon sketch on my parents' fridge.

So I chew the skin on my fingers
And pray this feeling will not linger
Because I can't promise
I can hold it together much longer
Breaking character
The role of a lifetime
It's my prime time
Never my time
But I guess I'll be fine

I'm always fine
On the outside.

Ghost

I don't know why I'm
So afraid of being judged.
I'm invisible.

Blemish

I like to think
Your words don't touch me
I don't even blink
At your disdain or cruelty

Of course, it's not true
Your jibes punch my skin
Bruises, mauve and blue
Without and within.

Trite

Tight lock
Ticking clock
Time flies
Tired eyes

Shit clichés
Shameful haze
Shallow words
Shackled birds.

Angst

It's an anchor
Chained to my ankles
Yet another
Pithy analogy
To analyse
Seeking answers
Visceral antipathy
Concealed anger
A curse of ancestry?
An anomaly?
Just another anecdote
Of endless anxiety
And the perpetual antagonist
Remains anonymous.

Splinter

You told me to be myself
With the silent
Yet crystal clear caveat
That 'myself' must meet
Your arbitrary stands
Or I'd find myself
By myself
Exiled and disgraced.

Disorder

Nonsense
The illogical ramblings of a
Mis-wired mind
Fact
Feeling
Intertwined
Seeking truth
In thoughts maligned.

Unmanageable

Grasping for the shiny cord
Trailing away behind another balloon
Floating away
Aching fingers
Stretching taut
Clutching the prize
Tying the cord to a brick, then
Snatching at the next elusive tail
Tiring now, I'm tiring now.
Losing sight of the tail
Turning to see the first cord
Slipping
Escaping
Weeping softy as balloons drift
Towards to sun.

Purgatory

I'm dead inside
I killed what was left
Destined to be worthless
No lasting connections
No one to remember me
No one to perceive me.

I have burnt every bridge
and refuse to seek out new ones
Matches in my pocket
Should a bridge appear in front of me.

I recoil from touch
I am vague, noncommittal
hiding
disappearing
forgetting
forgotten.

"Who am I"
becomes, "Am I?"

I am so completely dead
and so tragically alive.

Purpose

What should I do with my life?
What should I do with my year,
My month, my day?
The days add up
But nothing adds up
And I'm stuck
In this day,
This month,
This year,
This life.

Imposter

From thick, glossy paper
The girl smiles at me
Gaps between her teeth
Backwards cap over white-blonde hair
Denim shorts and a Minnie Mouse t-shirt
Mid-bounce on a trampoline.
Eyes bright
Skin unmarked
I remember being her
But I can't remember how.

Mind

It's more than a mood swing
More than 'one of those things'
My mind can snap from
Nothing To See Here to
I Don't Want To Be Here
Though I know nothing has changed
It's all the same life
I was living
Five minutes ago.

Something is different though
I can't put my finger on it
I just feel like shit
And I'm so wrong
I don't belong here,
There,
Anywhere,
It's all a blur and I can't see
A place for me.

So I hide and hope I'll disappear
But all I hear is

You'll never get away,
Not tomorrow, not today
The problem is you
And their problem too

It's all you, you, you.

Diagnosis

Anger is not always anger
Sometimes it's a mask
Disguising disappointment, even despair.

Those hurried, ten-minute conversations
Decide who I am
For the rest of my life.

Heaven forbid I protest,
The cold, unfeeling
Tap, tap, tap, tap - codifying my existence.

Any questions? No, good.
Because to question the label
Proves the label is unquestionably correct.

End

Soaked in the sweat of hibernation
Unstoppable train, run away
Insidious, intrusive
Churning, the fog grows thicker
I am no longer scared
Dry eyes
Absent
Let go, fade into the abyss.

Parched

My heart overflows
Brimming with love, but I sip
And it tastes of salt.

Truant

A faint chime, new text:
Just checking in, see you next
Friday? We missed you.

Dreams

The clock ticks backwards
Nocturnal, hiding in the shadows
The darkness comforts me
The silence soothes my soul.

I am alone
Lonely, but I don't care
I won't forsake my silent nights
When with open eyes my dreams come alive.

Crash

Double-down on the wreckage
It's unfixable, written-off
Slash another tyre
Added faults will not testify
Against your identity.

There is no need to register
A second event,
A third, or thirteenth
No follow-up paragraph
No context needed.

The committee follows the constitution
Simply nominating
A single item on the books
No torture, no preaching
Just one judgement, undeniable.

A disaster in countless parts
And they already accept that this
Will not be the last.

Insomnia

Exhausted, but I can't sleep
Distorted, now I can't see
The world smudges and shifts around me
Like I'm underwater and I can't breathe.

Flake

"Not today, I can't."
"But you said that yesterday..."
"I know, but... I know."

Succumbed

Aching fingers release
Let the paintbrush fall
It clips the table, crawls away,
Drops to the floor with a soft click.

Almost ready to give up,
Too many blank canvasses sullied
Delicate lines smudged,
Colours spoiled.

The bravest artist could not save them
And I am not a brave artist.

Insight

I know
What I do
I even know
Why
I just don't know
How to stop.

Glitch

A film reel
Replaying
Again, again, again.

A slideshow
Flickering
Stuck, stuck, stuck.

I close my eyes
But the frames
Click on.

Sprint

Go, go, go
Just blow through
This feeling won't last
Make the most of it now.

Bust.
It's gone.
It didn't last long
And I can't do a damn thing now.

Hologram

Gone.
Gone where?
Did I imagine
You were there
In the first place?
I hate
I can't trust my brain
I feel insane
What is reality?
It's real to me
But you can't see
And if you don't see
Does that mean
It's never been?
It's always me
Who must agree
I didn't see
You're right
I didn't see.

Frustration

Mind control both feared and sought
Someone else would do a better job.

I always chose the red counter
Accepting blue as second-best.
Never yellow, never green,
Red; the lucky favourite, I thought.

At least, I think I thought.

If I could go back
I'd swap out my piece
For a sprig of lavender
Or a smooth piece of rose quartz.

At least, I like to think I would.

Victor

Sometimes
The only way
To win the game
Is to refuse to play.

Futility

I know you're watching me
Waiting for me
To expose a secret
That doesn't exist.

You're grasping at straws
Pulling me down
Punishing me for something
I didn't do.

I have nothing to give you
I can't create a more palatable
Less painful narrative
I can only tell the truth

And I have.

Fall

As the leaf crunches under my foot
I imagine the problem
Crushed into tiny pieces
Floating away with the breeze
A brief moment of success
I have achieved
I am content.

Then I look up
And an infinite sea of orange and red
Still surrounds me.

Fly

I stand entrenched in thick, brown mud
My thoughts are poison to my blood
I sink, collapse, too weak to cry
But in my dreams, I swear, I'll fly.

The rain beats down, the waters rise
I pray for help, no one replies
Now all that's left to do is die
But in my dreams, I swear, I'll fly.

And yet, a spark, a glimpse of light
The stars remind me how to fight
I've more to do, I've got to try
For all my dreams, I swear, I'll fly.

Tarot

I don't trust a word I think. My brain and I don't have that kind of relationship. I envy those who do. I just don't think it's on the cards for me.

Cursed

I live inside a brain
That lies to me.
I can't trust myself -
Why should anyone else?

If they don't,
        They're cruel.

If they do,
        Stupid.

No one wins
The race was rigged
From the beginning.

Contract

Warning: Do not enter
Caveat emptor
Read the reviews and the product description
No refunds
Sold as seen
Can I be any clearer?
Don't come nearer
This refurbished item is not guaranteed
So don't waste my time
Oh please, don't waste my time.

Risk

Bittersweet lemons
A kiss to my lips
Poison to my wounds
But I can't have one
Without the other.

Walls

Curate the library of your memories
Remember:
Membership, once granted,
Cannot be revoked.

Withdrawn

I'm so afraid
Of saying
The Wrong Thing
I simply say
Nothing
But I think
That might
Be worse.

42

A decorative number
On a plaque by the front door
Roses and a pretty serif font
A portrait of what we want others
To believe is inside.

Transference

Weights on my shoulders
You shouldn't pass them to me
Rather, set them down.

Amplify

Don't play it down
It's not a lie, it's the truth
Your reality
Just explain what they can't see.

They're right though – it is all in your head
Your brain is sick, you might need meds
Some therapy to heal your wounds
Calibrate where you're untuned.

However, they make one mistake
You can't will this away, or pray
Prayer alone won't treat your injuries
No tinctures, herbs, or witchery.

You need help
Don't ask – demand
Shout until you're heard
Every pain. Every word.

Meaningful

A black cat walks down a grey street towards a brown house with a red door and silver doorknob.
Or was it gold?
The cat didn't notice.
The darkness feels heavy.
Yet darkness is only the absence of light.
Sunlight beats down.
Can you feel its weight too?
Space.
Stumble through the dense forest into a clearing that cradles a glistening lake.
Crystal.
Cold, empty.
Hot, full.
Are you my heart? Am I?
Correlation makes sense out of nonsense, but is that really what we want?
Does it matter what we want?
The glassy-eyed raven doesn't blink.
Look again.
Again.
Cold, empty.
Follow the winding path, even as it disappears.
Don't worry about getting lost.
You're already lost, for now.
Maybe forever.
Looking back to confirm you've left the path, realising the path was never there.
Don't run.

Whatever you do, don't run.
Walk, swim, play, sing, climb, dance, fall.
Stop.
Look around.
Can you see it all?
Can you see at all?
Take off the blinkers.
Walk away.
Shed a layer – I'll wear it, though it is heavy as the darkness.
Heavy as the sunlight.
Hot, full.
A dazzling steed or a burdened donkey.
I can always pretend, until I can't.
Neon camouflage.
Lipstick masks a split lip un til they lean in for a kiss.
Flinch.
They didn't split my lip, but their kiss feels like fire, reawakening the pain so carefully layered in scarlet and pride.
Eyes darting wildly, searching for the path.
There is no path.
There was never a path.
Run.
Don't run.
Run.
Cold, empty.
Stop running.
No one is following you.
Laugh.
Cry.

Laugh again.
Catch your breath, love, the worst is yet to come.
And the best.
Sit. Breathe.
The flames may strain to lick your skin, but you can extinguish them with a single breath.
So they say.
I try to believe, yet keep a stock of aloe.
Just in case.
I count the scars belief has etched on my body.
Look away.
If you don't look, it doesn't exist.
So they say.
That's a lie.
But the truth is heavy.
Heavy as the darkness.
Cold, empty.
The black cat meows softly.
The doorknob is gold.

Interpretation

It is not my job
To make it make sense to you.
Read between the lines.

Progress

Better,
But not normal.
What is normal? I ask,
Will I ever be?
Have I ever been?

Secrets

I promise I'm lying.

Teddy bears are sentient. Dolls are not. Anymore.

Purple doesn't actually exist. We are all seeing a different colour at the same time.

Clocks tick anti-clockwise, but our brains don't like it, so they flip the image, so it looks like the hands are moving clockwise.

The best cure for a broken heart is a haircut.

If you tell a lie, it will never come true, even if it was going to before you lied about it.

Your prayers are not being ignored. God's secretary, Joan, is just really behind with her emails. God was going to fire her, but she brings in cupcakes every Friday, so everyone in the office loves her and God doesn't want to be unpopular at work. That would be awkward.

Optimum depletion is correct.

My favourite office supply is the pink highlighter, followed closely by the paperclip. The pencil sharpener can go back to hell.

Twelve apples are too many.

I think, therefore, I think.

Make a mess. Clean it up. If you feel like it.

Sanity is relative.

Your passport will self-destruct when it expires.

Just play along - it will be funny, I promise.

Odd socks at the back of the drawer.

The pen is mightier than the sword, but only if the ink is blue.

We are all alone, together.

Be kind to the monster under your bed. They're your oldest friend.

Wake up. Please, wake up.

Nothing is a coincidence.

Don't pick up that penny.

If the soup is cold, pour it into your bag and go home.

Green parachutes are safer than red.

A haunted necklace, once worn, is difficult to remove. You won't want to.

Let the cup overflow, but don't let the bubbles touch the ground.

The invasion is scheduled for next month, but it's only pencilled in. We're still awaiting their RSVP card.

When a salesman produces a robin, offer him a cup of tea. The robin, not the salesman.

There is no incentive, only fear.

Tea for sorrow, coffee for joy.

You are a prisoner of your own hypothesis, a catalogue of irreconcilable differences.

A bronze medal is like an inflamed appendix.

Pluck a feather from the wing of a hero. Plant it in the ground and nurture it with love. Observe as your homegrown hero emerges from the damp soil.

Linger, don't loiter.

You are a guest, not a tourist.

One key on every piano is rigged to alert them that you wish to confess.

Empty bookshelves feel lonely.

Write your memoir on a chalkboard. Doodle in permanent marker.
Twelve months, three days.
That's your deadline.
Good luck.

Offline

There is a

Disconnect.

The world

And I.

I log on

To connect

But

The connection I find

Is not

The connection I sought.

I log off

To disconnect.

And I connect.

Discord

I am intelligent.
I am friendly.
I am competent.
I am logical.
I am brave.

I am naïve.
I am aloof.
I am dependent.
I am emotional.
I am timid.

I am enough.
I am excessive.
I am insufficient.

I am.
And I am not.

Weep

Angry waves in my brain
Crash behind my weary eyes
Yet the clouds won't break

Blue

Looking out at the Northern sky
I know this view too well
Can you tell?

When I've wandered
When I've fled
I've looked out and wondered

Is this the same moon?
Are these the same stars?
I know they are.

I am back.
The moon, those stars
Familiar as the hum of the cars
I hear from my childhood bedroom
Where I count the times I've landed
I've been stranded
In this room
Where I dare not roam
Where I dare not stay.

Hesitation

Pen poised over paper
In my restless left hand
Words snagged on the nib.

Paused, perched on the precipice
In a fog of sound and silence
A sharp poke to the rib.

Inextricable; restraint feels like violence
Inexplicable; dislodge the ink from the tip and
Write, right now.

Blossom

Sit next to me
Not too close
Maybe across from me
I am afraid, see.

I crave to be
A little less morose
Calm my bouncing knee
Share some herbal tea.

Gaze upon the hazel tree
Nothing grandiose
We find that we
Connect effortlessly.

Again

The old rabbit hole
Covered in crimson and gold
A romantic fall.

Abstain

I should probably cut you off
It's not that I don't think I can do it
I've kicked more than my fair share of vices.

Maybe that's the point,
I feel I'm owed this one vice
After all,
Life should not be all about restriction, right?

But I guess I said that about the drink too.

Remembrance

Surrounded by crumbling gravestones
Though yours was never here
It's all I have.

I pray spirits are free to roam
Lest you lie confined to that island
You never called home.

Do you have a grave?
Were you buried or burnt?
I'll never know.

The moment you left is seared into my brain
Flashing behind my eyelids
No sound – the machines were silent by then.

I tripped head-first into your empty plot
Waiting for you,
But neither your corpse, nor your soul, returned.

Tortured by the choices you made,
This is your story, but mine too,
And while you rest, I still remember.

Martyr

Self-sacrifices
Held to my throat like a knife
It was never love.

Spinster

Am I doomed
To be alone?
Am I doomed
If I'm alone?

Emptiness

I let you fill the cavities in my heart
With your empty words
Choosing not to acknowledge their banality
Better to pretend you see me
Than to feel there is nothing to see.

Vicious

I think I hate you,
Or at least, I can't stand you.

You're not as funny as you think you are
Nor kind
Nor smart
Nor selfless
Nor anything else you pretended to be.

I think I indulge you,
Or at least, I endure you

Because everyone else is more funny
More kind
More smart
More selfless
More everything than I can be – except for you.

I'm tired of trying to see the best in you,
The rose-tinted glasses cracked
And all that's left is this:
I don't feel like the worst person in the room
When I'm with you.

Canine

Almost duped anew
But I don't exist to stroke
Your fragile ego.

Thanks for reminding
Me how manipulative you
Still are. Not again.

Tail between your legs
You can't see the irony?
Bark away – I won't flinch.

Control

I forgot to collect my prescription.
I shake the transparent box
As if I can't see the white and peach capsules
They must be there.

A wave of sickness laps at my stomach
An elastic band snaps at my temples
My malfunctioning brain
Pre-empting what comes next.

The capsules promise me autonomy
Then, when it is just within my reach
A blunt reminder
I have a new master.

Myopic

Triangles printed on the side of a box
Notebooks with rose gold rings
The unbroken spines of books unread
A painted canvas from the time I let go.

Scratched desk
Wooden chests
Wires and wires and wires
Two screens, ever glowing.

Eyelids scrape the lenses
I crave a new view
With soft lighting and crisp air
Far away from here.

Recovery

When you're sure the DVD logo is going to hit right in the corner on target, but it glances the side and BAM she's off in the other direction. Frustration. Disappointment. Sadness? Not again. I was so sure this time.

Plan

Make the decision
Not to decide.
Cede control,
Find peace.

Possibilities,
Not probabilities.
Glance at the map,
Deviate at will.

Pack a bag,
Step, step,
Engage, enjoy,
Live.

Epiphany

I'm not sure I care what you think anymore,
Empty words don't hold the weight they did.
Falling flat, they inspire nothing
Except begrudged pity,
So, I walk on.

Perhaps all those words I thought so profound
Were empty shells,
Each step I take, another cracks.
Maybe they paved a way for me to move on,
So, I walk on.

When guilt arises,
Guilt for the trail of abandoned fragments
I think, I once would have picked up every shell
Keeping them safe in my breast-pocket,
So, I walk on.

You can't show me your shells are worthless,
Fragile, laid out like an assault course
Punctuated with snares,
Then ask me to keep picking them up.
So, I walk on.

Script

Conflicted.

My strength and shelter
An overbearing editor
My words erased and rewritten
In a voice I don't recognise.

I don't relate.

Should I stop writing?
Make the editor the ghost-writer?
I can't live like that.

Seeing is believing.

Unlimited trust in the editor
Is to limit myself
From the sights I've seen
The sights I want to see.

I need change.

I am the writer.
My words, my story.
I'll take the errors, the plot-holes,
The criticism,
Knowing they're mine.

My words are flawed,
But they are mine.

Punishment

My wounded soul resides
In a wounded body
Living in a wounded world
Yet I still chastise her
For being afraid.

Place

Maybe we're not lost
Maybe we're searching
For a home that won't exist
Until we stop looking
And build it.

Misguided

I don't want you to take my hand
To pull me
To push me
This direction
Or that.

I want you to sit with me
Help me take my own hand
To pull me
To push me
Any direction
I want.

Memories

Is this moment truly frozen in time?
Is it a single moment,
Or a composition, surreptitiously polluted?

Shards break away,
Fluttering away into the wind,
An urgency arises
Fingers strain as fragments dance like fireflies,

Always
Just
Too
Far
Away.

Wounds emerge and we stuff them
With scraps of paper,
Sticky notes and love letters unsent,
Once thick and crisp,
Later, a soggy pulp
Malignant rot infesting the heart.

Choice

Walking backwards into the future
No amount of cash will cover the insurance
Retire to the spare room, years too early,
Years too late.

A gift, disguised as a curse, disguised as a gift,
Soap cleanses and smells like bliss
More, more,
Never enough.

Prisoner. Stockholm syndrome,
The same breakfast each morning
Refusing sweet pancakes or buttered toast,
No thanks – this loop suits me fine.

Hostage to myself
Skills of restraint, finely tuned
Bound and withdrawn
From the freedom I claim to crave.

Kick

Treading water
All this effort, energy expended
To stay in the same place.

Head bobbing on the surface
Trying so hard
Yet staying still.

I've lost sight of all land
I can only imagine it
Far off in the distance.

If it's so hard to stay in one place
How could I reach something I cannot see?
Hope fades like the sunset.

I am lost
Afloat but stranded
Reserves depleting breath by breath.

Indecision is death
But can my weary arms
Strike out towards nothing?

Artefacts

I let go of your things
Some time ago
Clearing space in my mind and soul.

One crumpled photograph remains
Trapped behind the bookcase
Too heavy to move.

Unseen, ever present
Haunting to space between here and not-here,
One last remnant.

Perception

What if the light
For which I search
Is the one
I can already see?
The one from which
I'm told to run.

Chase

Like a grand piano on my chest
A deep, purple bruise, burst capillaries
I know I can't outrun you, yet run I must

Eyes dart
Embers crackle in my lungs
This flight must end.

Stop, turn
Show these demons my face
And fight.

Doubt

It's the waiting that gets me
I wait on you, and you let me wait
Then you're finally here and all I can think is
I hope you don't notice my sweaty palms.

Echo

What would you actually like me to say?
Should I format the words in a structured cliché?
Must I spell it as gray when I used to write grey?
Ought I alter the image I want to portray?
Need I tiptoe around you to dodge the affray?
Will I have to be silent to keep you at bay?
Would I risk ostracism if I disobey?
Could I brace myself for impending foul play?
Might I seek out my own path of soil or clay?
Am I ready to step out and go my own way?

Goodbye, yesterday.
Hello, today.

Release

I wonder if I'll wander
Somewhere to cast asunder
Any notions of devotions claimed
Under duress, reactive stress.

Could I let my mind be kind?
I'm not sure I know how, but now
My heart is set on needs unmet
Turning yearning into learning.

Spring

A daffodil in an April storm
She bends, contorts
But her roots hold firm
And though her spine may break
She will not.

Now

Grief, for what is not.
Relief, for what is no longer.
Belief, in what might be.

Ownership

I have a black dog
But now, I dress him in a
Colourful jumper.

Overwhelm

Forget-Me-Nots spill over the side
Of the plant pot on my cramped balcony
Overcrowded, starving, suffocating,
How could I choose
Which flowers to prune?
But I don't have a bigger plant pot.

Fit

A shirt from Shop A
A shirt from shop B
Though marked as the same size
Unlikely they'll be.

I'll fit into one
The other's too small
Somehow that's my fault
I should fit them all.

I'll all so subjective
With rules underpinning
I don't have the rulebook
The world just keeps spinning.

Baggage

Emptying out my backpack
Assorted items in a pile on my bed
When I consider what to repack
I catch sight of the stain where I bled.

So I scrunch up the backpack, embrace it
Then push it down into the bin
I'm finally willing to face it
I'm healing without and within.

I order a fresh, unused backpack
Deliberately choose what it holds
Set off to the unknown, a new track
To see how this journey unfolds.

Here

I like it here
It's unfamiliar, yet secure.

I like it here,
My thoughts are softer, less unsure.

I like it here,
And that's enough for now.

I like it here,
A cosy chair, a gentle meow.

Fog

My favourite kind of weather is fog. The fresh, crispness of the air; the blanket that seems to dull the noise. The feeling that everything and everyone has slowed down and lowered their voices. The feeling that all the problems of the world and The Others have been subdued and I am in a protected space. The fog is my shield, my comfort, and my hope.

Fear

I am afraid
Of doing
And not doing
Of being
And not being
But most of all
I am afraid
Of having
The decision
Made for me.

Less

I don't have much
I don't need much
The kaleidoscopic view
Has melted away
Clear, crisp
Comfort is not to be owned
But experienced.

Ethereal

It's that lighter feeling in my chest
This new day feels brighter than the rest
It may not be the best way
But I see it in a new way
It's just lighter
It's just brighter
Than before.

Consent

It's for me to choose
My boundaries aren't elective
My answer is no.

Ruminate

In search of dignity
Digress into silence
Communication with self
Captivating, elaborating on thoughts
Merely tolerated
Habits deteriorated
Guidelines ignored in favour of imagining
An unconducted orchestra
A tragic operatic, histrionic scene on repeat
Consecutive performances
A company never tiring
Just wait
Before an action irreversible
It is not necessary to burn down the theatre
Only to book a new act.

Sunflower

Growing strong
Though potentially precarious
My tall, exposed stem
Vulnerable to damage
Keeps growing
Focusing on my roots
My petals bloom
Reaching for the sky
Enjoying the view
And if I break
At least I'll remember
What I saw.

Tide

The waves are calmer now
A rhythmic pulse
Somewhat predictable
No more surfing
Simply floating
No more holding breaths
Simply breathing
Slowly
Deeply
Drifting steadily back to shore.

Meaning

Misty-eyed archangel
Eloquent in her silence
Advance, retreat
Narrow windows open to
Interpret her message
Nine sparrows and a robin
Give you a sign.

Intuition.
Senses.

Reveal your motive
Elaborate
Learn and grow
As the elder tree
Towers in full
Indomitable
View of
Everyone.

Someone
Only you.

Clear a path
Hope guides
Open your eyes
Open your heart
Sketch with ink, decisive,
Expect and experience.

You're a cub,
Older each day
Uproot the weeds
Rewrite the future.

Own your fate as
Winter fades into spring
Night fades into day.

Wanderlust

I've stepped onto a new path
Where the trees whisper in the breeze
Where the birds carry notes from afar
Where words hold meaning
Beyond their definition.

I know not where the path leads
Nor do I care
I'm just so thankful
To be on it.

Escaped

Now redefined and understood
Where once could not, I dare I could
I take this glimpse of hope and run
With glowing light, new life begun.

The road is long, with struggles more
But now with sparks inside my core
I never saw, but now I see
I'm not defeated, I am free.

Sensory

One step at a time
Leaves crackling underfoot
Autumn smells like joy.

Hush

This thick carpet of snow
Somehow feels warm
Softening the sounds of a chaotic world.

In the elements
I am in my element.

Brave

It is cold, not gloomy,
Hunkered down, no need for pretence,
Remove the costume
In favour of a heavy sweater
A magnanimous shroud
Offering peace over fear,
Tenderly cloaking your flaws
As you let them breathe.

Ensconced
Exposed
Protected
Vulnerable
Safe in your fragility.

I won't tell you not to fear
Bravery is not fearlessness
Bravery is courage in fear.

Frost

I wake to wintry air
Brisk, rejuvenating breaths
Flooding my veins with life.

The frost that kills the flower
Restores my spirit
Nourishing every cell.

How lucky I am
To be alive
For just
This moment.

***

Acknowledgements

This book would not have seen the light of day if not for some wonderful people in my life, to whom I am eternally grateful. I'd like to thank them here.

Firstly, I'd like to thank me. Thank you for finally being brave enough to make this book a reality. It took a long time, but you've actually done it. I'm proud of you.

My parents, Gillian and Mark, who have always believed in my writing and encouraged me to share it. For catching me when I fall, for holding me while I heal, for helping me to fly when I doubt my own wings. For this and so much more - thank you.

My brother, Dan, for always finding me the "anxiety corner", then standing beside me in it. For making me laugh when I thought I could never laugh again. Thank you for being my partner in crime. Oh, and I'm sorry I asked Mum when you were "going back" when you were a baby. And for dressing you up in oversized, novelty sunglasses. And for telling everyone about "the bathtub incident". Oh bollocks, I've done it again... Love ya, bro.

My former CPN, Michaela, for being the first mental health professional who went above and beyond to gain my trust and keep it safe. With her support, I was able to work through the pain to find a strength inside myself that I didn't know I had. Thank you for hearing all the things I couldn't say. Thank you for helping me to say them.

And finally, to all the people who probably have no idea how significant their kindness and support is to me, in helping me to be my true self in this strange world: Amy, Tanja, Cesca, Grozzy, and everyone who humours me on Twitter, whether I'm complaining, making bad jokes, posting old memes, or oversharing. Thank you.

About the author

 Hazel lives in Derbyshire, England.

What I Meant When I Said I'm Fine is her debut poetry collection.

When she's not writing, she can usually be found exploring weird internet rabbit-holes, volunteering at her local library, making lists, reading, napping, dad-dancing, living in a daydream, or tweeting nonsense into the void.

Her heart belongs to her cats: Anna and Elsa.

Twitter: @thepatchworkfox
Blog: www.thepatchworkfox.com
Email: thepatchworkfox@gmail.com

Printed in Great Britain
by Amazon

10503906R00068